Free as a

as a

Bird

THE STORY OF MALALA

Written and illustrated by Lina Maslo

BALZER + BRAY
An Imprint of HarperCollins*Publishers*

Balzer + Bray is an imprint of HarperCollins Publishers.

Free as a Bird: The Story of Malala
Copyright © 2018 by Lina Maslo
All rights reserved. Manufactured in China.
No part of this book may be used or reproduced in any manner whatsoever without
written permission except in the case of brief quotations embodied in critical articles and reviews.
For information address HarperCollins Children's Books, a division of HarperCollins Publishers,
195 Broadway, New York, NY 10007.

www.harpercollinschildrens.com

ISBN 978-0-06-256077-3 (trade binding)

The artist used acrylic and ink to create the illustrations for this book.   Typography by Rachel Zegar   18 19 20 21 22 SCP 10 9 8 7 6 5 4 3 2 1   ❖   First Edition

For my husband and children

"Don't ask me what I did.
Ask me what I did not do.
I did not clip her wings,
and that's all."

— Ziauddin Yousafzai,
March 2014

When she was born, people sighed and shook their heads.

"A girl," they whispered.

"What bad luck."

But her father looked into
her eyes and fell in love.

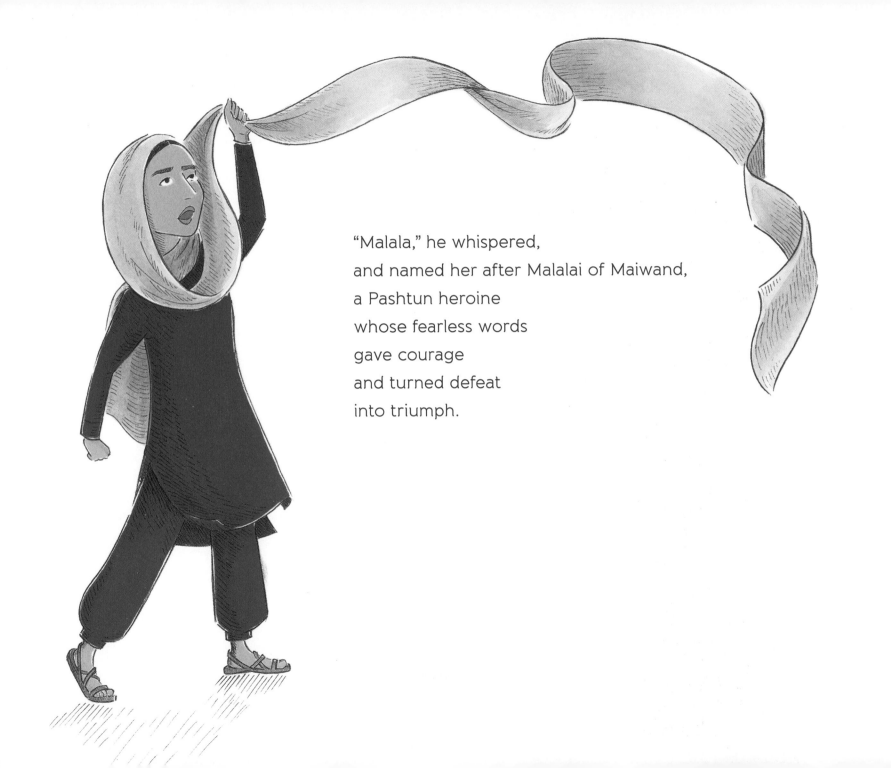

"Malala," he whispered,
and named her after Malalai of Maiwand,
a Pashtun heroine
whose fearless words
gave courage
and turned defeat
into triumph.

Malala's father ran a school for boys and girls.
He took her tiny hand into his
and led her through the halls.

Malala would sit in classrooms filled with older children,
and she would listen.

And before she could speak,
she would wander into the empty rooms
and teach.

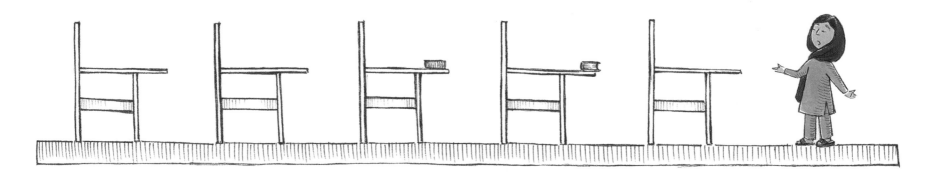

As Malala grew, she realized that women in Pakistan did not have the same rights as men.

Women like her mother had to hide their faces.

They were expected to marry young and have children.

They could not be anyone they wanted to be when they grew up.

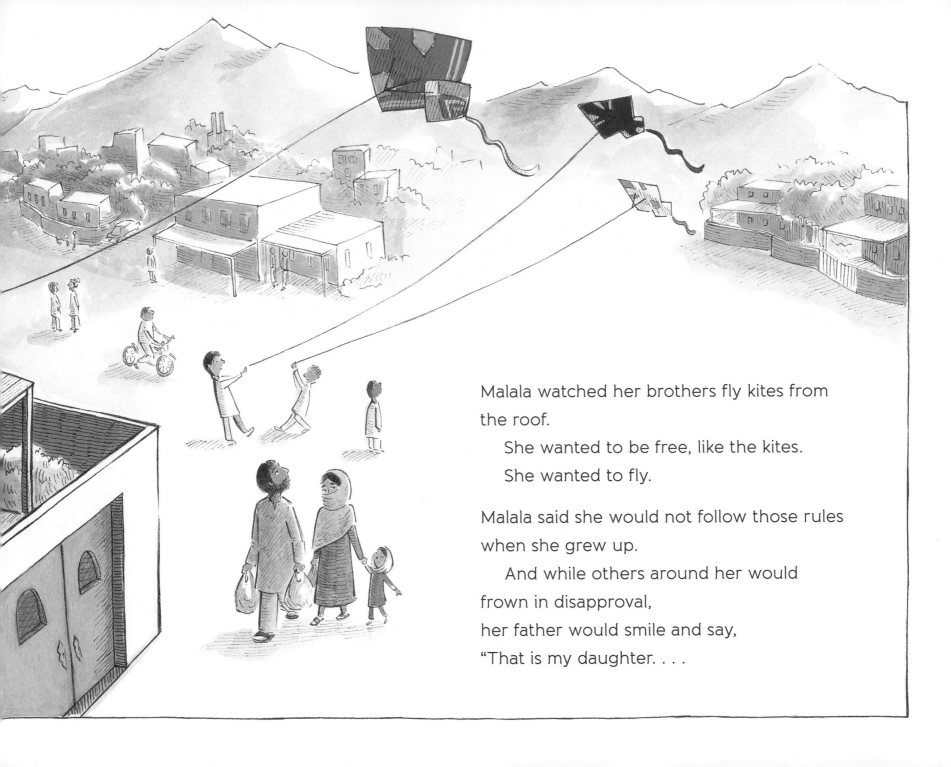

Malala watched her brothers fly kites from
the roof.
     She wanted to be free, like the kites.
     She wanted to fly.

Malala said she would not follow those rules
when she grew up.
     And while others around her would
frown in disapproval,
her father would smile and say,
"That is my daughter. . . .

"Malala will be free as a bird!"

And Malala did feel free
within the doors of her school,
within the covers of a breathtaking book,
within the patterned pages of calculus and chemistry.

She loved to participate in public-speaking contests at school and would often win.

Her father said, "You should be a politician."

Malala laughed, and shook her head.

She would be a doctor.

Her father said, "You could help create a society where *any* girl could become a doctor."

But then a new enemy came to Pakistan.

At first the enemy hid within the radio.
    They told the people what to do.
    They told the people that girls could no longer go to school.

Then the enemy came out of hiding.
    They punished people who did not listen to them.
    They blew up schools for girls.

The government sent an army to fight the enemy,
and a war began.

At night, Malala and her brothers hid in their
parents' room as the two sides fired at each other.

But during the day, Malala secretly went to school.

Malala's father was not afraid.

He spoke out and begged people to stand up to the enemy's demands.

Malala watched her father's speeches.

She said to herself,
"Why don't you go and fight for girls' rights?
Fight to make Pakistan a better place?"

Malala's mother said, "Speaking up is the only way things will get better."

So Malala began to talk about the importance of schools for girls.

"No one will stop me," she said. "I will get my education."

But the enemy began to threaten
Malala and her father.
    They told Malala's father:
Do not teach girls.

They told Malala: Do not talk about girls and education.

One day, Malala's father told her she should stop speaking out because it was getting too dangerous.

But Malala said,
"This is now my calling. You were the one who said that if we believe in something greater than our lives, then our voices will only multiply."

"I will protect your freedom, Malala," said her father.

"Carry on with your dreams."

But the day came

when he could not

protect

her.

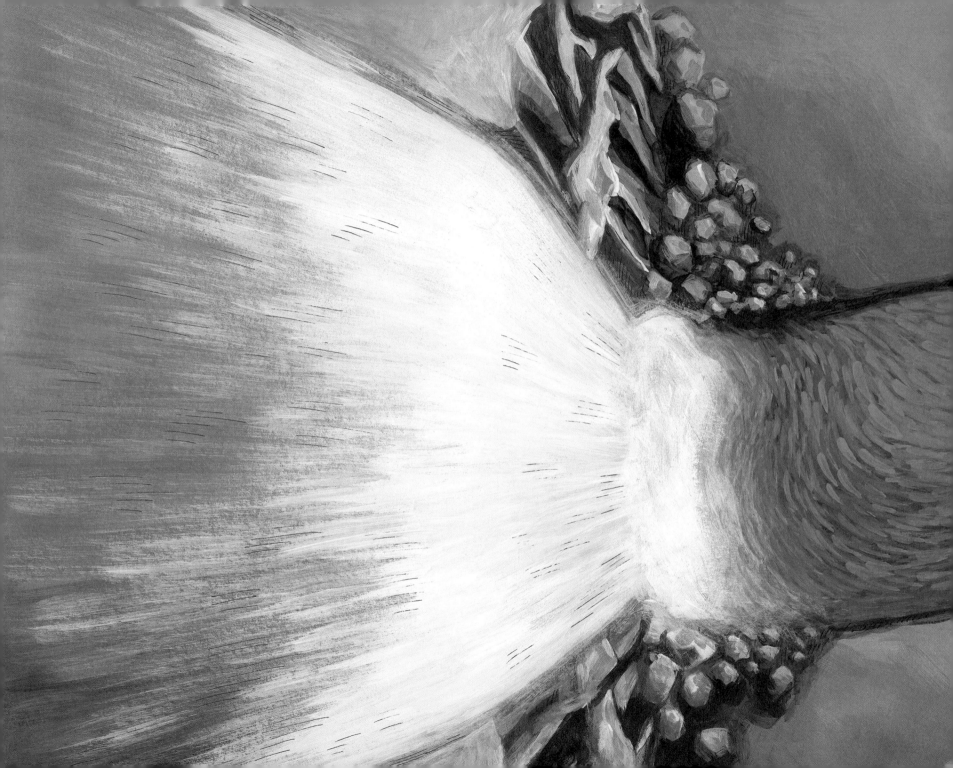

For seven days, Malala slept and dreamed. . . .

She awoke in a hospital.

She was told that the enemy had tried to end her life.
But she had survived.

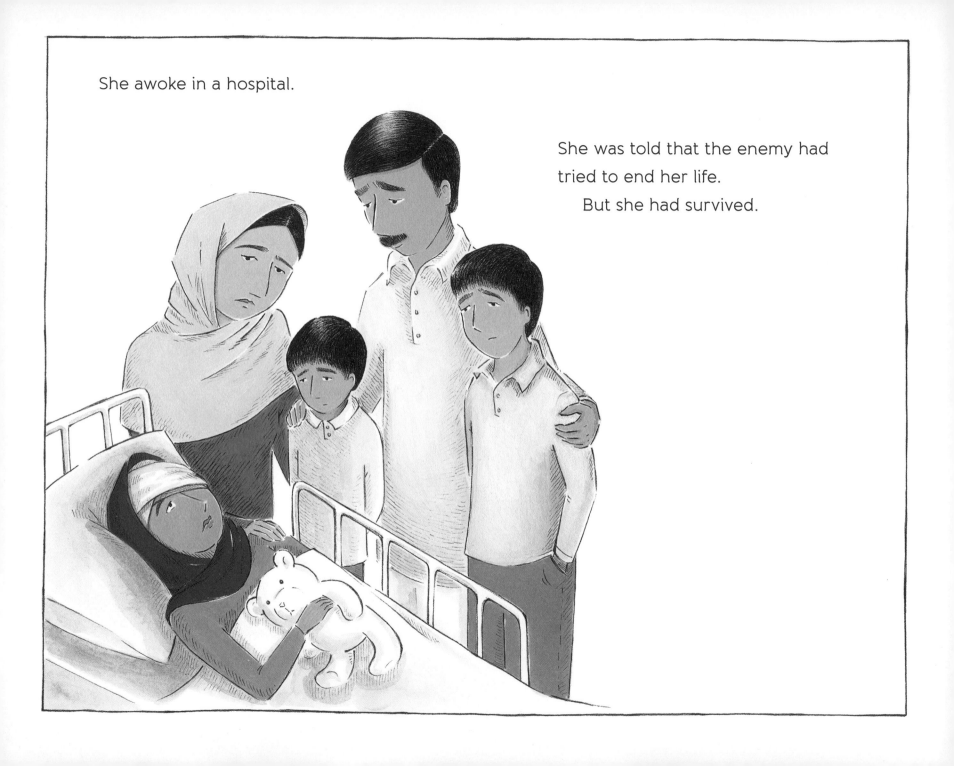

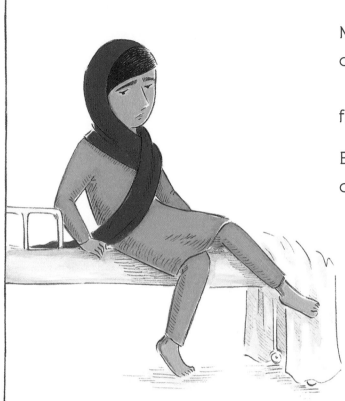

Malala was no longer in her beloved country of Pakistan.

She was now in England, where girls are free to go to school and learn.

But she knew that girls and boys in many countries could not.

Some of the countries were too poor.

Others were always at war.

And still others didn't think education was necessary, especially for girls.

Malala would not keep silent.

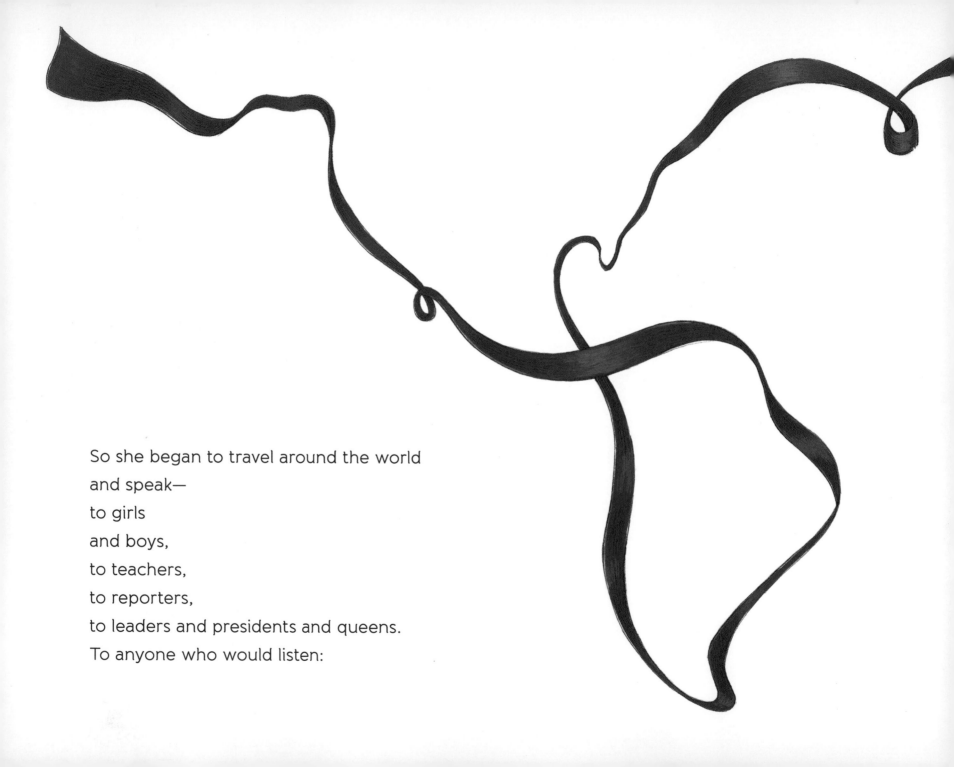

So she began to travel around the world
and speak—
to girls
and boys,
to teachers,
to reporters,
to leaders and presidents and queens.
To anyone who would listen:

"I speak—not for myself, but for all girls and boys.

I raise up my voice—not so that I can shout, but so that those without a voice can be heard.

Those who have fought for their rights:

Their right to live in peace.

Their right to be treated with dignity.

Their right to equality of opportunity.

Their right to be educated. . . .

One child, one teacher, one pen, and one book can change the world."

And Malala's father watched and said,
"Look at her! Don't you think . . .

. . . she is meant for the skies!"

"When the whole world is silent,
even one voice becomes powerful."

—Malala Yousafzai,
September 27, 2013

Author's Note

Malala Yousafzai was born on July 12, 1997, in Mingora, Pakistan, to Ziauddin Yousafzai and Tor Pekai, Sunni Muslims who are part of the Pashtun tribe. In this culture, a girl is expected only to marry and have children when she grows up and is not usually allowed to have a career. Education for girls is minimal, and their futures are limited. From the beginning, however, Malala's parents loved her and encouraged her to become an educated woman.

A believer in education for all children, Ziauddin Yousafzai opened several schools for boys and girls throughout Mingora. By the time Malala was eight, he had opened three schools with a combined total of over eight hundred students. He was also a respected leader in his community, and he often spoke out against religious extremism.

In 2005, after a terrible earthquake in Pakistan that killed over seventy thousand people, a *mullah*, or religious leader, began to make speeches on the radio. He insisted that the earthquake was Allah's punishment of the Pakistani people for not following stricter laws. He told people they needed to stop listening to music, watching movies, and sending girls to school. There was no reason for girls to go to school, he said, because all they needed to know was how to be good wives and mothers. He told the men to stop shaving and the women to wear *burqas*, clothing that covered everything but their eyes. After a while his followers, part of a group called the Taliban, began to infiltrate the cities and punish people for disobeying these new rules. They destroyed barbershops, music stores, and schools. By the end of 2008 they had destroyed over 150 schools for girls in Mingora alone.

Malala's family did not agree with these teachings. Ziauddin kept his schools open for as long as possible. He began to speak out, and Malala soon found her own voice as well. She began to talk to reporters from newspapers and TV shows. A BBC reporter came to the school and asked if any of the girls were willing to narrate a blog about their experience. So Malala began to speak to the reporter, who published the blog, titled *Diary of a Pakistani Schoolgirl*, under an anonymous name. Not long after, the *New York Times* made a documentary about the school situation in Pakistan, and Malala and her father were in the film. People soon found out that Malala was the author of the anonymous blog, and the Taliban began to threaten Ziauddin and Malala, ordering them to stop speaking out and to close the schools.

The Pakistan Army fought the Taliban for over a year and a half and managed to drive them into hiding. However, it was not enough to get rid of them.

On October 9, 2012, two members of the Taliban stopped Malala's school bus. "Who is Malala?" asked one of the men. As the girls all turned to look at Malala, the man shot her, injuring her and two other girls. Malala was treated in Pakistan, then flown to Birmingham, England, at the request of a doctor there. After being in a coma for a week, she awoke. She had been shot in the head.

After a long recovery, Malala regained her ability to speak and walk. Her father wondered if she would be the same Malala she had been before. She was, and on her sixteenth birthday, Malala spoke in front of the United Nations Youth Assembly in New York City.

Malala and her father cofounded the Malala Fund, a nonprofit organization with the goal of providing girls around the world with twelve years of quality education. Then, on December 10, 2014, Malala was awarded the Nobel Peace Prize. She is the youngest recipient of the award. Malala continues to travel and talk about the importance of education for girls and all children. She currently lives in Birmingham, England, with her parents and brothers, Khushal and Atal.

Timeline

1997—July 12: Malala Yousafzai is born in Mingora, Pakistan.

2005—October 8: Earthquake in Pakistan kills seventy thousand people. Maulana Fazlullah, the "Radio Mullah," starts to give speeches on the radio.

2007—Taliban infiltrates Swat Valley in Pakistan, where Mingora is located. The Pakistan Army arrives to fight them. War breaks out.

2008—Malala begins to speak to reporters about education for girls.

2009—Malala narrates the BBC Urdu blog *Diary of a Pakistani Schoolgirl*.
   —**January 15:** Girls schools close in Mingora.

2011—December 19: Malala wins Pakistan's National Youth Peace Prize.

2012—October 9: Malala is shot by the Taliban.
   —**October 15:** Malala is transported to Birmingham, England. The Malala Fund is established soon after.

2013—July 12: Malala addresses the Youth Assembly at the United Nations on her sixteenth birthday. It is named "Malala Day" by Ban Ki-moon, Secretary-General of the UN.
   —**October 8:** Malala's autobiography *I Am Malala* is released.

2014—December 10: Malala wins the Nobel Peace Prize along with Kailash Satyarthi of India.

2015—July 12: Malala opens the Malala Yousafzai All-Girls School in Lebanon for Syrian refugees.
   —**October 22:** The documentary *He Named Me Malala*, directed by Davis Guggenheim, is released.

Who Was Malalai of Maiwand?

Malalai of Maiwand, like Malala, was part of the Pashtun tribe, a group of people that stretches across parts of Pakistan and Afghanistan. In 1880, when the British tried to take over the country of Afghanistan, many of the local people began to fight against them. Malalai's father and fiancé both joined the battle. As Malalai was tending the wounded, she could see that the battle was being won by the British. She grabbed a piece of fabric—either a flag or her own scarf—waved it in the air, and shouted to all the men, "Young love! If you do not fall in the battle of Maiwand, by God, someone is saving you as a symbol of shame!" Malalai was killed by British troops that day, but her speech gave the Afghan fighters courage, and they won the battle. To this day, she is remembered in Afghanistan and Pakistan as a woman of courage and honor.

Further Resources

Books:

Brown, Dinah. *Who Is Malala Yousafzai?* New York: Grosset & Dunlap, 2015.

Yousafzai, Malala, and Christina Lamb. *I Am Malala: The Girl Who Stood Up for Education and Was Shot by the Taliban.* New York: Little, Brown, 2013.

Yousafzai, Malala, and Patricia McCormick. *I Am Malala: How One Girl Stood Up for Education and Changed the World* (Young Readers Edition). New York: Little, Brown, 2014.

Films:

Class Dismissed: The Death of Female Education: Malala's Story, by Adam B. Ellick and Irhan Ashraf, accessed March 6, 2016, http://www.nytimes.com/video/world/asia/100000001835296/class-dismissed-malala-yousafzais-story.html

He Named Me Malala. Dir. Davis Guggenheim. Fox Searchlight Pictures, 2015.

Websites/online articles:

www.biography.com/people/malala-yousafzai-21362253

"Diary of a Pakistani Schoolgirl," accessed March 6, 2016, http://news.bbc.co.uk/2/hi/south_asia/7834402.stm

www.malala.org

"Malala Yousafzai's speech at the Youth Takeover of the United Nations," accessed March 6, 2016, https://secure.aworldatschool.org/page/content/the-text-of-malala-yousafzais-speech-at-the-united-nations/

"Nobel Lecture by Malala Yousafzai, Oslo, 10 December 2014," accessed March 6, 2016, www.nobelprize.org/nobel_prizes/peace/laureates/2014/yousafzai-lecture_en.html